WHAT IS YOUR STRATEGY FOR GOOGLE, FACEBOOK AND AMAZON

A CEO's 10 minute brief on staying ahead of the competition and making sure you have the right partners

What are the three biggest threats to your revenue in the next 18 months?

While there may be a variety of industry or niche-specific concerns impacting your business, this book is focused on three main threats to your revenue over the next 18 months:

1. Larger sites and big box stores are driving up paid search costs and benefiting from recent algorithm changes in organic search, making it more difficult to acquire quality traffic.

2. Amazon and other marketplace sites are driving down margins and enabling increased competition from manufacturers and suppliers.

3. Internal marketing staff, SEO and pay-per-click agencies are struggling to keep up with the evolving marketplace and maintain ROI levels.

So, client acquisition costs are going up, you're working harder than ever, and you're not sure if your "expert" resources are doing everything they can to help you. Sound about right?

What can you do about it? Over the last four years, we have tracked the performance of thousands of small and mid-size ecommerce businesses and interviewed the CEO's of the top performing 1% to find out what they do that is so different. Here are the top seven strategies that set them apart:

Strategy Number One: Identify where you're weak

In our practice, we work with hundreds of CEOs and understand that everyone has their own opinion about the relative value of outsourcing vs staffing internally. Most business owners make an effort to staff up internally around functions that they perceive to be core competencies of the business. This logic generally works well, as full-time employees give you more control and oversight on their work, as well as a better opportunity to retain the accumulated knowledge from that work if they ever leave or are terminated.

If you operate a business that depends on the Internet for a substantial portion of your leads and revenue, it is easy to extend this basic thinking to online marketing functions. Depending on the size of your company and the amount of revenue coming from online efforts, you may have a single person managing your site and campaigns or a small team of internal people. While it may make sense in very large companies to completely in-source online marketing support, for the vast majority of businesses it simply isn't the best strategy. There are three reasons successful companies outsource to compete online:

Rapid platform evolution

The platforms on which you market your products and services (Google, Facebook, LinkedIn, etc.) and the entry points to them (paid ads, content, re-targeting, mobile apps, etc.) are evolving and changing at a rapid pace. Best practices, strategies and ad programs are becoming increasingly complex and specialized, requiring more time and effort to stay competent from an administrative point of view. Lack of awareness or involvement in new programs can also mean lost opportunity and lost revenue.

Accelerated training requirements

Because of the rapid changes in the platforms themselves, the amount of training required to stay at the top of the game is increasing dramatically. The amount of time one person would have to spend getting trained and staying current on all the various aspects of online marketing would easily eat up their entire week and leave no time to actually do the work you hired them to do. Professional marketing firms can spread the cost and utilization of this kind of training across a broad set of clients, making it feasible – whereas you simply cannot.

The use of specialized software

As the platforms and marketing channels continue to evolve, the need to monitor brand assets, coordinate content and optimize ad buying across those channels is becoming more critical. Many agencies have developed specialized software to aid them in these processes, or pay large licensing fees to use commercially available tools, giving their clients an edge over less sophisticated competitors. The use of these applications is often not possible or prohibitively expensive for many small businesses.

These dynamics are driving a large increase in outsourcing, especially around more technical services. While it may make a lot of sense to have core FTE's managing content creation and product inventory, it's a good idea to make a realistic assessment of their skills and identify areas where you are stretching their capabilities. If they just don't have the skills or the training cost is too high, it might be time to find outside partners.

Strategy Number Two: Focus on ROI - not cost

Whether you are dealing with internal staff or outside contractors, the biggest mistake we see CEO's making on a regular basis is focusing on budgets or cost over ROI.

Successful owners start by asking the right questions:

Power Questions:
- What will it take to increase our sales in this area by X% over the next 12 months?

- Given our size/position relative to our competitors, how much do we really need to invest to effectively compete? In which areas (SEO, paid search, affiliate, social, mobile, etc.?) should we be focusing our investment?

- Given my product/service set, current positioning and budget, what are the highest ROI activities we should be focusing on?

- How can we ensure that as we go down the road, we quickly eliminate non-performing activities and focus our dollars on profitable ones? What metrics should we use to identify them?

- What is a reasonable expectation of overall ROI for the investment I'm making?

Those are the kinds of questions that will lead to a blueprint for success, rather than simply a list of things that will be done for a given budget.

Playing to win

The reason this is important is because people often wonder why they don't get the results that they want. Generally, this is because they aren't asking the right questions. They focus on a budget figure rather than getting an accurate picture of what investment is needed to create positive ROI. You are competing directly against other companies that are investing in the same kinds of services, so understanding where you need to be positioned relative to them is critical. Many companies fail because they invest too little or try to take on major competitors with too little ammunition. Your trusted advisors will tell you when you're under-sizing the task, but there are always people willing to take your money and give you false hope that you can succeed, when really they know you can't.

If you are using outside contractors to assist you, you also need to calculate the additional costs on your end to support the work the vendor is doing. You may need to spend additional staff time to augment their efforts and implement their recommendations. It's important to factor these costs into your overall budget as well as your ROI calculations, so that you get a true sense of the return. The right way to think about it is: "What do I need to invest in a program so that I win? So that I become relevant enough to attract clients and build significant ROI?

Let's say you were going to enter a marathon and were talking to a trainer and you said, "I want you to train me for the marathon but I'm only willing to spend two hours a week training." A trainer who is desperate for the money and doesn't really care will say, "OK, sure. I'll work with you for two hours. I will put together a plan and we can get started next week." On the other hand, someone who really knows what they're doing will look at you and say, "You might as well not waste your time, because you'll never even finish the race if you don't commit at least 10 hours a week to the training process – and I don't coach people that won't finish."

We have a client who runs a professional services firm and when they first came to us, they were doing about $1,000,000 a year in online sales. Sales had been flat for over a year and they were looking for ways to move the needle and increase revenue. When we spoke to them originally, we talked to them about what they were trying to accomplish (their campaigns, etc.) and the CEO was adamant that he wasn't willing to increase his budget. They had a vendor in place that had been working with them for the last two years and he felt that the amount that he was investing was an amount that he wasn't willing to increase.

We really got into a deep conversation about what his objectives were and as we really defined his goals for growth, it became very clear to us that he needed a different kind of partner. He needed a partner that could do more comprehensive work than the company that he was with currently and that that work was going to be more expensive. In fact, it was going to be almost double the budget that he was currently spending.

The conversation really turned to ROI vs budget. Over the course of these conversations, we were convinced that he could see significant increases in sales by adopting a different strategy with a different partner, but it would require an additional investment. Ultimately, he took our advice and decided to go with the company that we recommended. The additional cost was $3,000/month over what he was paying before, but with the new program in place his sales tripled. If you figured it on an ROI basis it was almost a 900% return - obviously a win for him, but would never have happened if he'd stuck with a fixed budget.

Strategy Number Three: Set clear expectations

After hiring and managing hundreds of employees and negotiating hundreds of marketing services contracts, we've identified two areas that are most often responsible for bad contract relationships:

Lack of specific service deliverables

Depending on the type of employment or outside service you are contracting for, there are usually a set of specific deliverables associated with it: amount of content to be created, products managed, ROI, budget spent, etc. A lot of times these items are discussed verbally but never make it into a contract. This is really on the owner, since employees and most companies default to leaving this kind of detail out of contracts so that they have more wiggle room down the road.

Power Questions:

- How can I quantify the work that you are doing? What specific work and/or activity is expected to be done every month?

- After the first phase of implementation, what are the things that I'm going to be receiving on an ongoing basis?

Lack of specific communication expectations

This is a big one. How often will they talk to you? In our experience, the best outside companies have regular, planned communication with clients which allows them to update you on progress and learn about any new developments on your end that may impact what they're doing. Vendors who say they are there "when you need them" or that communication "depends on what's going on that month" may be sincere, but being specific up-front sets the tone for a productive long term relationship and creates a clear expectation that can be referenced if there are problems with the account manager later on.

Power Questions:

- Who will I be talking with on a regular basis and how often will we be communicating?

- What should my team prepare for these scheduled calls to make them more productive? What information from our end would be helpful?

Strategy Number Four: Focus on the account manager rather than the salesperson when contracting

Falling in love with the salesperson

If you have contracted for marketing services in the past then you know that some of the worst companies in this space have the best sales people.

They know exactly what to say and are excellent at selling the big brands and major experience of their firm. In the sales process, they will promote that they work with Honda, Nike, IBM, etc. and dazzle you with their experience and white papers, most of which are about companies much bigger than yours, i.e. the ones that they put their really smart account managers on. If you focus on this aspect of their pitch, you'll probably be thinking "Wow, these guys must be really good. After all, Honda wouldn't work with schmucks."

They build rapport and confidence with you and convince you that everyone on their team will be just as good as they are and care deeply about your account. Now, we're not knocking legitimate salespeople and the work they do, but a lot of companies in the online marketing space have adopted a business model that specifically focuses their resources on sales at the direct expense of service, because they believe it is cheaper to acquire new clients than it is to retain them. This is the "churn-and-burn" model at its best (or worst). This is why we strongly recommend vetting the actual account manager before signing a contract, because when all is said and done, they are the one you will be dependent on for results.

The importance of account manager selection

As part of the build-out of our national network, we have evaluated thousands of companies and hundreds of individual account managers within those companies. We went into the online marketing companies and actually invested the time to understand the account management structure and its impact on performance. Here's what we learned.

99% of the success of your relationship with an online marketing company will be determined by your specific account manager. What often happens is that when the sales manager closes a new account, it goes into a lottery system for account manager assignment based on which of their staff have the most availability. And guess who usually has the most availability? Newer, less experienced account managers who don't already have a full book of clients. This is especially true if you are a small business client in a large agency.

Account managers drive your experience and results

It may seem obvious to say that not all account managers are created equal, but our experience has been that most companies have very little formal, ongoing training or fixed procedures related to the communication cycles and work which account managers put into individual accounts. This results in an extremely high correlation between campaign performance and individual project manager assignment.

After evaluating the performance of hundreds of campaigns, we found that account managers who consistently ranked at the top end of the scale not only increased the performance of the campaigns they were responsible for, but also retained their clients longer. Communication was more frequent, follow-up was better and clients were generally happier.

So how do you get a good account manager?

Ask for one. More specifically, tell the vendor that you need to know who your account manager will be before you sign a contract. Talk to them, interview them and look up their background. What are their values? What's their skill set? What's their experience? Ask them specific questions about your website and what their plan is to help you improve it. If you don't like the answers, ask for a different account manager up front.

> **Power Questions:**
> - What experience do you have with the specific services I'm contracting for?
> - What training or certifications do you have?
> - Have you worked on similar-sized accounts in the past?
> - What is your plan to increase revenue for my business? Why?
> - What's the best way for us to communicate?

What if you think you have a bad account manager?

Demand to switch. You should do this immediately. Wasting time trying to make a bad account manager better isn't your problem - it's a training issue that the vendor needs to address. You should never be shy about calling the senior manager at a vendor and asking for a new account rep if you're not happy.

The big lesson here is that it's fine to evaluate the company you're going to contract with, but if you don't evaluate them down to the individual account manager, you are risking the performance of your entire campaign. Don't be dazzled by their client list, white papers and PowerPoint decks - focus on the people that will actually be doing the work for you.

Strategy Number Five: Learn to identify the bad apples fast

Like most things in business, you get a gut feeling for whether the things that your vendors are doing are legitimate and are being done right. You don't need to be a technical expert, but you do need to know enough to know when you're getting scammed. Here are some red flags to look for and how you can identify trouble before it gets too far down the line.

Lack of Transparency

The first red flag is lack of transparency. This takes many forms, such as when a vendor says that they're creating content for you but they won't show it to you. They may reference articles or blogs that they've created but won't send you copies for review and approval. They may make changes to the actual content on your site but not offer you detail on what changes were made and when. Some will even claim that they've built links to your site without disclosing which sites they are on, saying that it's part of their "proprietary process".

Access to Accounts

Access to accounts is another dangerous red flag. If a vendor says that they've created accounts for you - especially Google AdWords accounts or other advertising accounts – but they won't give you access to them, you should be worried. They may tell you that they are managing them under their "internal system" or as part of their "master account" and can't give you access - don't believe them. If you're paying for third party ad services, you need access and control over those accounts; not just to monitor the money, but to retain the valuable intelligence from historical data in the account if you ever fire the vendor.

Bogus Reporting

The third area of common abuse is reporting. There are reporting platforms which are specifically designed to allow vendors to create confusing reports that mask a lack of performance. SEO is an area where this is most often abused, and we often see vendors sending out reports that are either intentionally confusing or outright fabrications. The bottom line is that you are smart enough to understand any report that's legitimate. Don't be intimidated to ask questions and make them explain every part of the reporting to you... and if the explanation doesn't make sense to you, there's probably a reason.

We had a client come to us and say: "I think my marketing company is doing a good job, but I'm just not seeing the sales increases I should be." When we asked why he thought that, he showed us a report from the vendor showing that he had had 65 "conversions" on his paid search campaign last month, which the vendor said were completed sales from clients who had clicked through on paid ads. "But the number of sales on the site last month was only 43 in total," he explained. "I just don't know why things aren't adding up; I mean, the numbers from Google can't be wrong, can they?"

So we called the vendor and started asking direct questions about the "conversions" tracking they were doing and also asked for access to the AdWords account. It turned out that there were some "mistakes" which had been made with the tracking pixels and that the real conversion numbers were much lower. They couldn't explain exactly what the mistakes were or why they had been reporting numbers which didn't match up to the actual Google Analytics for months.

Needless to say, this vendor relationship was short-lived and we got the client into a relationship with a reputable company. He now understands his reports clearly and can match them up with real sales every month.

The bad apples

Like any market, this one has bad apples. Unlike other markets, they can be a lot harder to spot.

The fact is that there are a lot of churn-and-burn companies which spend all of their energy strategizing around how to sell, mislead and retain you with little or no focus on actual performance. The really bad ones actively engage in tactics and practices that can be harmful to your business in the long term.

Getting on the right side

The long-term strategy for your business online should be based on best practices and on alignment with the interests of the platforms upon which you are advertising. If you ask the right high-level questions, they will lead you to the right conclusions: "Does the strategy we're pursuing benefit the end user?" "Does it make for a better experience for the person coming to the search engine or the website?" If you maintain focus on these questions, it's easy to tell when someone is recommending something that might get you in trouble down the road.

Ethical companies attract ethical employees and will talk about things like alignment, best practices and guidelines. They don't use words like gaming, tricking or masking and don't suggest that you create junk content or engage in partnerships with affiliates which aren't above board. They don't make lofty promises and they don't make guarantees about things they don't control. Avoid the temptation of things that sound too good to be true; focus on the right questions and listen to your gut.

Strategy Number Six: Be careful who you take advice from

Good intentions, bad advice

As you evolve your business strategy over time, you have to be conscious of who you're asking for advice. If you're working with an outside firm that is heavily geared towards social media marketing, they're likely to believe that the thing you should be spending your money on going forward is, unsurprisingly, more social media. The same thing would be true with a pay-per-click company, an SEO company, an affiliate marketing company and so on. Given this truth, it's critical that you find ways to get input from people who don't have a vested interest in one specific type of service or marketing platform.

It's important for business owners to get some outside opinions about the total strategy that they wish to implement. Just asking their vendors how they should be approaching things is clearly not enough, because the vendors are obviously biased towards the types of services that they provide. It's not out of malice; it's purely because that's what they know. That's what they believe in, otherwise they wouldn't be in that line of work.

Aside from specific vendor bias, it's also important to be aware that the market is constantly changing. In earlier chapters we talked about ROI being the metric that's most important. As you track ROI, it is often the case that as the months go on, certain types of activities will start to drive higher ROI than others. It may be in your best interest to move investment dollars from one type of activity to another. Unfortunately, if it means losing a contract, most vendors won't be eager to highlight that to you.

Search for the highest ROI use of funds

As the owner, your question shouldn't be: "Can I make positive ROI on this activity?" The power question is:

"Is this activity the highest ROI activity available to me right now?"

Those are very different questions. If you're asking the latter question, it forces you to look at everything and evaluate the potential returns that you could be getting. If you're asking a vendor or someone who is specifically involved in one aspect of online marketing, they're very likely to tell you that they think that the thing that they do most often is the answer... which it may not be. This is also a question which should be asked broadly in the business and put up against other offline marketing opportunities like print and direct sales.

One of our clients is an e-commerce specialty products company that came to us spending five figures a month on pay-per-click ads and $3,500 a month on an SEO company which was doing content marketing work for them. We looked at the overall investment that they were making, the performance of their campaigns and their blended cost of traffic. We ended up recommending that they reallocate their content marketing budget into a contract with a new vendor for a special type of technical SEO work and restructure their paid search program. The result of those changes was that organic traffic increased 35% in 90 days, representing an additional $30,000 a month in sales. By lowering their blended cost of acquisition overall, they were able to be more competitive with their paid search campaigns as well, expanding their reach into new ad networks and increasing ROI.

Getting quality outside advice and perspective on your marketing programs can be a challenge, but is well worth the effort.

Strategy Number Seven: Learn to manage integration

As the owner of the business, it is ultimately up to you to create integration between internal resources and contractors. How well you do this has a big impact on the leverage you get on the dollars you invest in online marketing services. Here are some thoughts and best practices we've built around integration.

Communication loops

There are two communication loops you need to establish with an online marketing partner:

- A regular, scheduled call to review reports and discuss upcoming activity. This call should include your internal marketing staff – and your staff should be prepared with questions.
- Direct, impromptu communication via email and phone directly between your staff and your vendor account manager when new products/services are launched, changes are made to the website or seasonal specials or events take place.

The account manager you're working with probably has at least a dozen other clients and has a unique point of view about best practices in different areas that are relevant to you. They also work with a team that has even more clients, so they have exposure to a lot of different practices and ideas that could potentially benefit you. That's a lot of information which you could get just by asking. Most people don't ask.

Here are some good open-ended questions to ask your vendor partner when you talk with them:

> **Power Questions:**
>
> - "What are the best practices for this type of work?"
>
> - "What are you seeing that is working with your other clients?"
>
> - "What trends do you see emerging in the last couple of months that are relevant to our business?"
>
> - "What do you think we could be doing to increase our conversions?"
>
> - "If you were in our shoes, what would you be doing that we aren't yet?"

Leverage

We often see CEOs leaving their vendors on an island. They believe that the vendor is responsible for obtaining certain results, but don't really put effort into using their own resources to increase the level of activity. In the case of online marketing companies, it is very often the case that a client will be paying for a defined amount of work to be done every month - content, page revisions, campaigns created, etc. If you adopt an approach geared towards leveraging your vendor's intelligence and your own resources, you can start asking questions like:

Power Questions:

- "What can my team be doing to accelerate your work?"

- "What would you recommend we do more of if you had access to my team's time?"

- "In what way can our team be more involved in the online marketing campaign so this campaign has a higher chance of success?"

- "What things can we be doing on a monthly basis to complement your efforts?"

Working to absorb best practices and industry knowledge from a vendor not only improves the campaigns you're working on with them in the short term, but also helps to retain that knowledge in your organization after the vendor is gone.

Create a team mentality

When you finalize an agreement with a new partner, begin integrating them into your team. Build communication cycles that involve them in your internal planning calls. Treat your account manager at the vendor company like part of your staff and get them invested in the outcomes you're trying to drive. When they commit to doing something with your entire team, you can be sure they will give it a high priority. Remember that people work to make money – but they work harder when they feel accountable to people they like.

Share vital information

Help your vendors do their job by sharing critical data with them. Sales, conversions, specials and new product and service data give them material to work with. The act of sharing information breeds trust and common accountability to shared goals. It also helps protect against a vendor hiding bad performance data or covering up mistakes.

Practical tips

Here are some other ways you can leverage your vendors experience and expertise:

- Learn how to read analytics yourself and ask detailed questions about your traffic and conversions.

- Get some of your internal people Google-certified so they can understand what the vendors are doing and ask better questions. This is not very hard or expensive, but gives you a big edge in the long term.

- Make sure that bi-weekly or monthly calls are happening and that your team comes prepared with specific, well-thought-out questions.

Stay Connected at the top

The final recommendation we have for you is to make sure you talk to the CEO of each of your vendor companies at least once a year. Tell them about your experience with their team as well as your goals for your business going forward. Ask them what thoughts and experiences they can share about your market or general trends that might be affecting you.

Simply scheduling a call with the CEO will trigger him/her to review your campaigns, get a status update from their team and make everyone downstream aware that you are directly communicating with the boss. It also gives you visibility at the top and puts you front-of-mind with the senior executive who may have other introductions or recommendations that could benefit you.

Why we wrote this book

As entrepreneurs ourselves, we have a very personal connection to the challenges of growing a business. We've spent years in our own businesses learning the market, hiring, firing, making money, losing money and struggling to keep up with the rapidly changing landscape of online marketing and e-commerce. We have also struggled with deciding when to hire internal staff or outsource and how to effectively manage contractors and their work.

Driven by our frustrations with these sorts of challenges, we came together in 2013 and founded Grow Team, the first national quality and performance vetting service for online marketing companies. Our idea was simple: find the best specialist agencies in the country, help companies get great deals with them and make sure they perform on the back-end. Since inception, Grow Team's experts have evaluated and thoroughly vetted more than 3,000 online marketing companies and helped hundreds of small and medium-sized businesses contract with them for services. We are the first true buyer's agency for online marketing services and have been growing our national presence at a rapid pace.

This book is our way of sharing the knowledge and experience we've gained from negotiating hundreds of online marketing service contracts with a large group of business owners.

People often ask us: "Doesn't giving away your knowledge undermine your business?" Definitely not. By telling people about what we do and sharing our experience, we will certainly help some people manage this process for themselves, but we will also inspire a lot of other people to call us and ask us to help them improve their businesses and take advantage of the thousands of hours of work we've already put into researching and negotiating these kinds of contracts. Either way, we are furthering our mission of helping business owners become more educated buyers of online marketing services.

About the authors

David Moses

David Moses is an experienced executive with a history of leadership roles in both early stage entrepreneurial organizations and established private equity backed groups.

He has a deep experience in building sales programs, increasing online revenue, building brands and improving operations through a disciplined, metrics-driven approach.

David is passionate about helping other business owners succeed in a rapidly changing business environment and dedicated to the long term success of our clients.

Originally from New York, David has two amazing daughters - and resides in San Diego. David has served on several industry boards, and was chairman and board member of the charity, Gift for Life.

Max Helmer

Max Helmer is a senior executive with experience in all aspects of early stage company growth. He has an in depth understanding of the online and digital marketing industry, as well as SaaS applications.

He has a broad base of experience in negotiating and managing contracts with outside suppliers, focused on generating long-term performance and results.

Max was born and raised in San Diego and loves working with small business owners to help them grow their companies.

Want to talk to us?

We help companies find the best partners at the best price. If you'd like us to evaluate your business and tell you what we think, just give us a call and tell us that you read our book.

Grow Team Main Office

800-741-9298

Or Visit

www.GrowTeam.com

Copyright © Grow Team 2018

Published by Grow Team Inc., California, USA

First edition published April 2016

All Rights Reserved. No part of this book may be reproduced or utilized in any form or by any means, electronic or mechanical, including photocopying, recording, or by any information storage and retrieval system, without written permission from the publisher.

GOOGLE is a registered trademark of Google, Inc.
AMAZON is a registered trademark of Amazon, Inc.
FACEBOOK is a registered trademark of Facebook, Inc.
Grow Team is not endorsed, sponsored or affiliated with or otherwise authorized by Google, Inc., Amazon.com, Inc. and FaceBook, Inc

Made in the USA
Columbia, SC
14 October 2018